CURIOUS CATS/ GATOS CURIOSOS

By Katie Kawa

Traducción al español: Eduardo Alamán

Gareth Stevens
Publishing

Please visit our website, www.garethstevens.com. For a free color catalog of all our high-quality books, call toll free 1-800-542-2595 or fax 1-877-542-2596.

Library of Congress Cataloging-in-Publication Data

Kawa, Katie.
  [Curious cats. Spanish & English]
  Curious cats = Gatos curiosos / Katie Kawa.
      p. cm. — (Pet corner = Rincón de las mascotas)
  Includes index.
  ISBN 978-1-4339-5590-7 (library binding)
  1. Cats—Juvenile literature. I. Title. II. Title: Gatos curiosos.
  SF445.7.K3918 2011
  636.8—dc22

                                              2011003607

First Edition

Published in 2012 by
Gareth Stevens Publishing
111 East 14th Street, Suite 349
New York, NY 10003

Copyright © 2012 Gareth Stevens Publishing

Editor: Katie Kawa
Designer: Andrea Davison-Bartolotta
Spanish Translation: Eduardo Alamán

Photo credits: Cover, pp. 1, 5, 9, 13, 17, 21, 23, 24 (meat, string) Shutterstock.com; pp. 7, 19, 24 (claws) iStockphoto.com; p. 11 Hemera/Thinkstock.com, p. 15 Fuse/Getty Images.

Printed in the United States of America

CPSIA compliance information: Batch #CS11GS: For further information contact Gareth Stevens, New York, New York at 1-800-542-2595.

Contents

Contenido

Cats like to play. They play with balls of string.

Los gatos son muy juguetones. Juegan con bolas de estambre.

Cats love to smell a special plant. This is called catnip.

A los gatos les encanta oler una planta llamada nébeda o catnip.

Cats are afraid of the water. They do not like baths.

Los gatos le tienen miedo al agua. A los gatos no les gusta bañarse.

9

A cat licks its fur.
This keeps it clean.

Los gatos se lamen el pelaje. Esto los mantiene limpios.

A cat needs food every day. They need to eat meat to stay healthy.

Los gatos necesitan comer todos los días. Los gatos comen carne para mantenerse sanos.

Cats go to an animal
doctor. He is called
a vet.

Los gatos van a un
doctor de animales.
Este doctor es un
veterinario.

A cat has pointy ears.
They help it hear sounds
far away.

Los gatos tienen orejas
puntiagudas. Esto les
ayuda a oír muy bien.

Cats have claws. They
use their claws to climb.

Los gatos tienen garras.
Los gatos usan sus
garras para trepar.

A cat makes a sound called a purr. This means it is happy.

Los gatos hacen un sonido llamado ronroneo. Esto quiere decir que están contentos.

Cats sleep a lot.
They often sleep for
16 hours!

Los gatos son muy
dormilones. ¡Con
frecuencia duermen
durante 16 horas al día!

23

Words to Know/
Palabras que debes saber

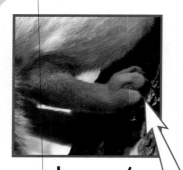

claws/
(las) garras

meat/
(la) carne

string/
(el) estambre

Index / Índice

24